# The Son Always Rises

## 31-DAY DEVOTIONAL

# Correne Constantino

ISBN 978-1-0980-9784-4 (paperback)
ISBN 978-1-0980-9785-1 (digital)

Christian Faith Publishing, Inc.
832 Park Avenue
Meadville, PA 16335
www.christianfaithpublishing.com

Printed in the United States of America

# Home Isn't a Place

Last night, I was lying in bed, unable to sleep, and I started thinking about "home" and how we use this word. What does it really mean?

When I go back up to Washington, where my family is, where I grew up, I say, "I'm going home." But when I come back to Texas, where I live, I also say, "I'm going home." When I'm staying at a hotel for a few days, sometimes, I even find myself saying, "Let's head home," after an outing or adventure. And finally, when I think of heaven and where I will be when I die, I think of my ultimate "home."

Dictionary.com gives us several definitions:

1. The place where one lives permanently
2. The family or social unit occupying a home
3. A place where someone flourishes

When I looked up Bible definitions for the word "home," I found one very interesting: "To be among one's people."

Maybe that is what it is all about...the people we are surrounded by, not the building or the city. Home is the people filling it! That is why our home is wherever we are, surrounded by God and the people we love here on earth: our people.

# Jesus Is a Sunrise

The sun peeks above the horizon, spilling its beautiful, powerful light over everything. Its rays touch the trees, kiss the grass, and awaken the birds, and it signals the start of the day. The sun rises without fail, without prompting, with consistency. And with each sunrise, a new day is born.

Jesus is a sunrise! Jesus, the light of the world, came to earth. (We call it Christmas!) As He came, He brought hope and love that touch everything and signal new life. His mercies are new each morning (Lamentations 3:23). He consistently and faithfully forgives our sin, renews us, and loves us as consistently as the sun comes over the horizon each morning.

Jesus isn't just a light like the sun. His light is eternal and holds so much more promise to us than the ball of burning gas we call the sun. The sun has an end; it will eventually burn out. But Jesus is the light of the world that will never die, burn out, or leave us in darkness. Jesus doesn't ever leave us in shadow like the sun does each night. His love is forever.

Romans 8:38–39 tells us, "For I am convinced that neither death nor life, neither angels nor demons, neither the present nor the future, nor any powers, neither height nor depth, nor anything else in all creation, will be able to separate us from the love of God that is in Christ Jesus our Lord."

Luke 1:78–79 reads, "Because of the tender mercy of our God, by which the rising sun will come to us from heaven to shine on those living in darkness and in the shadow of death, to guide our feet into the path of peace."

Jesus is the light! He is an eternal sunrise!

# IDENTITY

In our culture, we often identify ourselves by our career. I know that "teacher" was always a definition I leaned on. Teacher defined me. I taught in the classroom for fourteen years and had dreamed of teaching from the age of nine. So teaching was fully ingrained in me. But when I left teaching (in the traditional sense) and took a year off to be a stay-at-home mom, I lost my identity. I felt so lost and unable to "find myself" or define myself. It was such a strange place to be, and I never realized how tied I was to the title "teacher."

So often, we rely on our jobs, our culture, our background, or even our family name to define who we are. But those things are just words, labels. They don't make us who we are. If your label is stripped away, what are you left with?

The first step in our journey of defining who we are or discovering our identity is to dig deep, to the core, to the beginning, to the Creator. I was created with purpose. I was created with love, in the image of my creator, God. I am His daughter. And so were you; you are created with a purpose and in his image! You are also the daughter of the King (Jeremiah 1:5; Ephesians 2:10)!

The foundation of our identity starts with knowing who the Creator is, that we are His masterpiece, and we are created with purpose.

Father God,

Thank you for creating me in a unique, purposeful way. You knew me and had a plan for me, even when you created the sea, the sky, the creatures, and the lands. You are the Creator, and you have a plan. Each day, Lord, I want to live for you—living out my purpose. Help me to rest in the comforting fact that I am a daughter of the King! Amen.

# What Is Faith?

Faith can be explained by believing in and relying on something we can't see. We have faith that the TV will turn on when we push play. We have faith that our car will start each morning. Children have the most pure and perfect faith—they have faith in us! They know that we (their parents) will be there when they wake up, will feed them something for breakfast, will pick them up from school, etc. They have blind faith and often don't ever even think about what would happen if all of a sudden, we weren't there anymore. Faith for them has no doubts!

In the Bible, Jesus says that our faith should be like that of a child!

Matthew 18:3 reads, "And he said: 'Truly I tell you, unless you change and become like little children, you will never enter the kingdom of heaven.'"

Our faith in God should be unshakeable, unquestionable, strong, and child-like! We need to know one hundred percent of the time that God is in control. That God has a plan. That God will be beside us through rough waters. However, we stumble...we lose that faith...we doubt...or we try to be the ones in control.

The great news is, that is when God shows us his grace! We stumble, and he dusts us off so we can start again. So when you find that your faith isn't so child-like, thank God for his grace, dust yourself off, and reanchor your faith in Him!

# ENCOURAGEMENT NEEDED

Who needs encouragement? All of us! Kids need encouragement to get their homework done or finish their vegetables. We might need encouragement to get our workouts done each day and stick to a healthy eating plan. People need encouragement to achieve goals, to achieve work targets, and sometimes, encouragement is needed to just be a good parent.

We have an internal need to hear that we are doing a good job, and that we can keep going. We need to know that there are others going through the same things we are. We need to know that we are not alone. Our first source of encouragement should come from our Heavenly Father—through prayer, relationship with Him, and His word. However, sometimes, we also need it from our friends, family, inner circle, church members, etc. It is called fellowship! It is when a group of believers come together and talk, lift one another up, pray for each other, and commune together. It is vital for our Christian growth! And the best thing about it…"Where two or three are gathered in my name, there I am also," says the Lord in Matthew 18:20.

Today, find a way to encourage. Pray that God uses you to be an encouragement to someone today. Reach out in prayer (for someone), write a note, make a phone call, stop by, and visit.

> Therefore encourage one another and build up one another, just as you also are doing. (1 Thessalonians 5:11)

# Prayer for True Joy

Dear Lord,

True joy is found only in you! Joy is knowing that we will some-day be in your presence for all eternity. It is knowing that no matter what we face here on this earth, it is temporary. You have overcome all temptation, all fear, all illness, all sin, and all evil. You defeated death and the devil when you died on that cross for me and rose again three days later. You stepped in to be the sacrificial lamb in my honor. So now, when God looks down on me, He sees me through the perfect lens of Jesus Christ. That brings pure joy!

Oh, Awesome God, thank you for your love. It's a love that none of us can even begin to comprehend. It is a supernatural love that our earthly minds can't even explain or understand. But we know from your word that it is unending, it is undeserved, it is a gift, it is overpowering, and it is meant to be shared! That kind of love should bring us *all* the joy!

And Lord, you sent us *you*. You gave us the gift of the Holy Spirit to reside right inside of our hearts/souls. The all-powerful, lov-ing God resides in us. And with God in us, when we live in Him, we submit our own desires to His. When we truly allow Him to guide our feet, our mouths, our lives, we have the power of God. There is nothing here on earth that can stand against us. Nothing can snatch the Holy Spirit away from us. The Holy Spirit resides in us and brings us joy (and all the other fruits of the spirit). When we have Christ in us, how can we not have joy!

Lord, help your joy to shine through us. Help us to push aside our fickle emotions, our shallow thoughts, our fear…Help us to push aside everything that gets in the way or hides the true joy that we have in You so that pure joy shines through to the world. Help us to share *you* through our joy! In Your precious and holy name, we pray. Amen!

# FREE OF ACCUSATION

Colossians 1:22 tells us, "But now he has reconciled you by Christ's physical body through death to present you holy in His sight, without blemish and free from accusation."

Who criticizes you the most? Who judges you the harshest? Who puts you down with untruths?

If you are a child, you might name a child on the playground a bully, a boy/girl with a crush on you who teases to get your attention… but as an adult, the answer is very different and a very real problem. It's ourselves. We are our own biggest critic, bully, and enemy.

When you look in the mirror each morning, what is your mental dialog? Think about it and be real…do you criticize yourself for your blotchy skin, frizzy hair, extra weight around the middle? Do you beat yourself up when you try to button up those jeans that are just a little too tight? Maybe the gray hair is peeking through, and it makes you cringe inside. What is your biggest self-critique?

Would we ever allow anyone to talk that way to our children? Would we even allow a friend or stranger to speak to us like this in public? Why do we berate ourselves so easily and so harshly?

Jesus's death on the cross changed everything for us! He became our sin. Our sin died with Him so that when God looks down at us, He sees us through the lens of Christ. He sees us as wonderful, sinless, new, and fresh—clean.

We need to teach ourselves a new truth. When we look in the mirror, we need to see God's perfect creation, His child, His masterpiece. We need to see a clean slate, a fresh chance to radiate God's love, mercy, and forgiveness to the world. We need to see ourselves through the lens of Christ—forgiven and loved and created with a purpose! What words will you speak into the mirror today?

# SET FREE

In my distress I prayed to the Lord, and the Lord
answered me and set me free. The Lord is for me,
so I will have no fear. What can mere people do
to me? (Psalm 118:5–6)

"I called to the Lord and He set me free..." Wow! When I read this
verse this morning, I had to go back and read it several times over.
My heart lightened, a smile broke out on my face, and I took a huge
deep breath! When I call upon the Lord, He answers and sets me free!

What does that word "free" mean to you?

The first image that comes to my mind is almost "movie-ish"—a
scene of a person shackled to the brick wall of an old building (maybe
a dungeon), head hung in defeat, breathing is labored, hopelessness
surrounds...

The next image I see is modern-day parent...tied to a job, working long hours, running errands, cleaning the house, trying to give
children what they need but scrimping on the time they really need
and deserve. The hopeless routine that circles and continues; never a
way to break free because bills and unexpected expenses continue to
build. An unbreakable trap of today's world.

Then I begin to think about people who live in the prison of
their own mind. Maybe pain, maybe loss, maybe incredible heavy
burdens, unworthiness, hopelessness, depression, anxiety...the dan-
gers of an overrun brain or soul.

God can free you, whatever your situation, ailment, stress, or
trap may be! Call out to Him, allow Him to take control of your life.
Listen to His direction, seek His counsel. Read the Bible, and listen
to His desires for your life. When your desire matches His, life is full
of peace and fulfillment!

# TRUE PEACE

What does peace look like to you? When we daydream about peace, we usually think of a remote location—full of beauty, quiet, and breathtaking. The beach, the mountains, a lake…

Do you ever visualize peace in your living room? Kitchen? I know some moms (including me when my daughter was little) found peace in their closet even if it's just for a minute or two. A place of calm and quiet can rejuvenate us. But peace may seem hard to come by in our everyday life.

The truth is that peace is always within reach because it is inside of us. In Philippians 4:7 it says, "And the peace of God, which passes all understanding, shall guard your hearts and your thoughts in Jesus Christ." The peace of God is a gift to us through the Holy Spirit. We just need to be still, focus on Him, and find it. Peace on purpose.

Life doesn't usually give us much peace—from the chaos of getting ready in the morning, work, homework, chores, dinner, practice, rehearsals, grocery shopping, laundry, etc. There isn't much time or focus on peace. Yet, I think it is something that all of us long for throughout our day; am I right? I'm going to start choosing to take a minute or two throughout the day to let go of the stresses, the deadlines, the demands, and focus on Christ, His love, and His peace. I know that when I do, it will refocus my attitude to joy and gratitude, and it will help me to let His light shine brighter through my words and actions.

I challenge you to do the same; take a moment today to find peace on purpose. See what a few moments with God can do to change and improve your day and your peace.

# BROKEN BY FEAR

Fear is such a powerful yet unexplainable thing. I've seen fear change people, and I've seen fear chase joy out of any situation. I've seen fear disable people. Fear is a spark that turns into a roaring fire that spreads and rages through a mind or body. Often, fear has no roots, reasons, or causes. Fear can break a person.

Fear is a scary thing if it cannot be tamed, contained, and put out. How does fear affect you? What fear do you have that stops you from living your full life? Maybe it is a fear of failure? A fear of success or money? Maybe you have a fear of being alone or a fear of depending on others? There are all kinds of crazy types of fears that the devil breathes life into! They start in our mind, often as just a stray thought, a self-doubt, a worry, but we allow the devil to blow on that little spark of fear and turn it into a full-blown fire!

The good news is, the Bible has some pretty powerful messages regarding our fear and how to extinguish it. God says that when we believe and have faith, there is no room for fear. The phrase "do not be afraid" is written in the Bible 365 times! (That's one a day!) One of my favorite verses is from 2 Timothy 1:7 that says, "For God did not give us a spirit of fear (timidity), but of power and love and self-control."

We are not created to be afraid, to live in fear…instead, we have the power of God within us, and therefore, we need to walk with the confidence of His strength and wisdom! Turn your eyes to your Creator, remember who is in charge, and remember that the battle has already been won (Romans 8:37)! When we can live a life focused on His love, grace, mercy, and truth, it diminishes the fears that live inside of us. His love banks the fire that rages.

Help us, Lord! Put out our fears with your love! Help us to seek you in times of fear, and allow your promises and your truth to be a stream of water, smothering the fire of our fears. Amen.

# FEELING STRONG

Feeling strong isn't just physical. Working out every day helps my body to feel strong. I know that I can do things physically that I've never been able to do before, but that isn't what strength is all about.

Strength must start from within. Where does your strength come from? Is it how tough you can be mentally or emotionally? Are you strong because you can control your emotions (I never cry; therefore, I'm tough)? Are you strong because you never give up? Does strength come from working through problems? Success? Money?

We cannot measure our strength by looking at worldly, human things…those things will all disappear! Our strength (physical, emotional, and mental) can all be taken away or broken.

Our strength comes from God. Knowing God, learning His word, obeying His commands, trusting fully on Him, and submitting ourselves (humbling ourselves) is what gives us true strength. Sounds weird, doesn't it? To our earthly, human ears, it might…be humble to get strong?

How does that work?

It is actually very simple. When we humble ourselves, God is the strength. He provides the strength in our stead. God's strength and power are within us! Can't get stronger than that!

Do you want to be strong inside and out? Start with God's word! Go to church, join a Bible study, read the Bible! You'll be stronger than you ever thought possible because you'll feel the power of God working within you!

# 8 Definitions of Grace

The gift of grace is so beautiful, the meaning so simple, and yet it is so hard to be gracious to ourselves.

Let's begin by looking up the word *grace* in the dictionary (Dictionary.com). Did you know the word grace has eight different definitions?

Grace is a prayer before a meal.

Grace is an elegant way to move.

Grace is a charming characteristic.

Grace can be a privilege or special favor (approval).

Grace has a meaning of pardon or mercy.

This word is loaded with meaning. When it comes to God's grace, I think it is a beautiful word, heavy-laden with love. Grace from God holds forgiveness, mercy, favor, and His presence. Grace is a gift that He gives to each of us. This grace washes us clean from sin while asking nothing in return. His grace is a fresh start each morning. The grace from God makes us whole and encourages us to live a life of love for Him and those around us.

When we live in His grace, we can freely give grace (forgiveness, love, mercy, etc.) to those around us and ourselves. We will always fall short, we will always disappoint, we will never be as good as we wish we could be, and that is why there is grace! Beautiful grace!

# HILLS AND VALLEYS!

We are afflicted in every way, but not crushed; perplexed, but not driven to despair; persecuted, but not forsaken; struck down, but not destroyed; always carrying in the body the death of Jesus, so that the life of Jesus may also be manifested in our bodies. (2 Corinthians 4:8–10)

Life is full of hills and valleys. Some of our valleys are deep and wide while others are easier and quicker to traverse. As we travel through these times in life, we need to remember that God is with us in the valleys! He is walking by our side and holding us up as we stumble and fall. Each time that we face challenges and troubles, hard times, and pain, he is forming us into who we are meant to be. He is giving us a testimony.

The most beautiful testimonies can come from the most tragic, hurtful times in our lives. What are you going through right now? What struggles are taking place in your life? Is there a relationship with a loved one that is broken or damaged? Is a family member sick and suffering? Are you facing financial struggles that make you feel you are drowning? Look for God in this situation! Lean on Him, trust Him, allow your weakness to show His strength! And share! Share your testimony with others because He can use you to bring others to Christ!

# THE SIMPLICITY OF GOD'S LOVE

Do you ever struggle with a puzzle? Like a crossword puzzle? You think and think about what the word is…you know that you should know it, but it just won't come to you. You keep coming back to that one word that you just can't come up with. Then you ask someone, and they say it…and you can't believe you didn't think of it yourself! It was just too simple. Sometimes the simple, obvious answer is the most difficult.

That is how God's love is. I even believe that is how Christianity is. We overcomplicate it. We think, and we think…we try to answer all the questions and try to explain the miracles. Unbelievers especially…they try to pick God apart, figure him out. They want to unravel everything, and they want everything to be explained. It all just seems too big, too complicated. The letters just don't fit into the space if you'll continue with my crossword analogy.

But really…it's just so simple! Sometimes, maybe too simple, for those looking on, to even believe or grasp.

It's all about God's love. His love is the answer. It seems simple. But it's His love for us that allows us to love Him and be saved. He sent His son to die on the cross for us (in our place) because of His *great* love. The gift for us is eternal life; love! All we have to do is accept it. Accept His love and forgiveness. Believe in Him. It's that simple! Too easy?

God loves you! It doesn't matter if you've messed up and sinned. It doesn't matter if you aren't worthy—none of us are. It doesn't matter…*you* are loved. Simple! Will you love God back? Will you accept His love and forgiveness?

# WAITING...

I've never been good at waiting. I like to be in action. I like to have a purpose. I am driven and goal-oriented. Waiting is just not something I know how to do very well. It seems like wasted time or time that could be used in another way.

Do you ever feel that way when you are waiting for an appointment or waiting to meet someone who may be running late? In today's world, we have cell phones that do amazing things and allow us to even work, play, or be social while waiting. But do you remember, not too long ago, when waiting meant just waiting...sitting... being still...nothing to do?

Sometimes, God tells us to wait. We might be looking for a new job, trying to have a baby, wanting to get married, looking into colleges, wanting to retire, or simply needing direction in life. But God says, "Wait." He doesn't usually give us a reason or a timetable. We are asked in that moment to trust and keep going with life as it is in the moment.

The waiting can be painful, especially if it affects your finances, comfort, or family life. Waiting isn't supposed to be easy. Sometimes, that is the whole point; God wants to challenge us in some way, or He is waiting to align other lives with ours. It's a much bigger plan than we could ever imagine, and therefore, there is only one thing for us to do: *trust*!

In the waiting...trust! Believe and know that God is working. He is hearing you. He is moving, but it is in His time and in His way, not ours. But guess what? His way is *always* the best way! His way can be unexpected and mind-blowing. So trust and wait!

> Let the morning bring me word of your unfailing love, for I have put my trust in you. Show me the way I should go, for to you I entrust my life. (Psalm 143:8)

# AFRAID OF BEES?

My daughter is afraid of bees...deathly afraid. When a bee flies around her, she freaks out—she screams, cries, runs...she becomes almost hysterical. And there is no reasoning with her or calming her. It is a true phobia. And she's never even been stung before.

Do you have anything in your life that makes you afraid? Anything that worries and stresses you? That each time you have to deal with it, it drives you down into the dumps? Mine is the struggle of money.

What do you do with that struggle? When faced with a new situation (a bee buzzing around), what do you do? Do you allow it to stress you out? Do you lose sleep? Do you allow it to consume your thoughts and worry about it all day? That is very easy to do. I find myself being consumed until I find a solution.

Whatever your area of concern, take it to God. What would your day (your life) be like if you could take those struggles, that worry, that one sensitive subject, and let go of it completely. Act in obedience to God, walk in faith that He is in complete control, and that He will take care of you and the situation. Your focus then remains on Him and not the problem. You can live a life (a day) knowing that you are free because of His ultimate sacrifice for you. You can find *joy* in His creation and His love.

The next time you start to be overtaken by worry, consumed by fixing a problem, or overwhelmed by life, give all of it to Him! Read your Bible, pray, sing praises, talk to another believer...and let God be in control!

# Look Up!

A child sneaks a cookie out of the package and is caught by Mom. He looks down at his feet in guilt and shame.

We think back on our biggest mistakes and hang our head in shame. We are caught in a lie and can't look our spouse in the eye, so we bow our head down.

We sit in church being convicted and feeling sorry for the sin we've lived in; we hang our head.

See a pattern…sin, shame, guilt—we hang our heads. *But* I say, *look up*! We are getting it wrong! The only forgiveness, mercy, and grace come from above! When we need a fresh start, when we've sinned, and when we need forgiveness and mercy, we need to *look up* to Him, who is full of grace.

Step outside, look up at the heavens, take a deep breath, and say a prayer, asking that the Holy Spirit prompts you to *look up* throughout the day. Keep your eyes focused on what is above.

> Surrender your heart to God, turn to him in prayer, and give up your sins—even those you do in secret. Then you won't be ashamed; you will be confident and fearless. (Job 11:13–15)

# FAITHFULNESS IS A
# BEAUTIFUL WORD

What a beautiful word packed with meaning and promise! When I think about faithfulness, I think of consistency. I think of something or someone who never fails, who is always there. I think of dedication and promise. And I also think of the word "faith" on its own—believing in something without doubt.

Faithfulness is God! He is unfailing, unfaltering in His perfect love for us. He is *always* with us without fail. He is *always* loving and true and full of grace and forgiveness. And that will never change—that is faithfulness.

We are called to be faithful also—faithful to God, following Him only and completely and never doubting His love and plan for our lives. We are to be faithful in our love for our spouse (faithful in marriage), and faithful to our calling from God; faithful in carrying out His plan for our life.

How would you rate your faithfulness? Think on your life, habits, and focus. Are you faithful to God in all things? In your marriage and to your family? In carrying out God's plan and calling for your life? Take time to pray that God would reveal ways for you to be more faithful. Ask Him for help! And don't forget to thank and praise Him for His faithfulness to you!

# GOD LISTENS...

He hears your every word—spoken and unspoken. He understands your situation no matter how complicated. He stands beside you through all things.

Prayer is a powerful, wonderful thing. You may think it is one-sided, but it is not. As you pray, there are so many powerful, wonderful things going on. First of all, when you pray, you are praising, thanking, and worshipping as well as petitioning. You have an opportunity to glorify and thank God for the amazing miracles and opportunities he blesses you with daily. He hears you!

As you pray, you are building and establishing a relationship with the Father. You are getting to know Him more, you are building trust, and the Holy Spirit is working in you and through your prayers. A relationship with Him changes everything; it helps you keep Him as your focus, it helps you to stress and worry less, and it gives you more peace and understanding. It just changes your perspective and allows your life to match up with the plans that God has for you.

And God hears you. He listens to your pleas and your thoughts, your worries and your doubts. He aches to answer your prayers, and He does answer—always! Sometimes, we think prayers go unanswered, but they don't. Remember, they most likely won't be answered with a simple yes or no, but often, with a maybe or a wait! All of His answers are according to His timing; His time, not ours.

Pray today! Pray every day! Pray in all circumstances! He listens!

# ONE TRUE LOVE

Do you believe in true love? Love at first sight? I love a great love story! In fact, Hallmark channel is my favorite, and I love their movies year-round—Christmas, Fall Harvest, June Weddings, whatever...I am a sucker for a good, wholesome, sweet, love story (with a happy ending).

As great as our human love can be, perfect love doesn't exist between a man and a woman. There are always flaws in our relationships because we are sinful people. We may bicker, and we may disagree on finances or the way to raise children. We may argue about schedules and routines. We let one another down (he didn't take the trash out again?). We may hold spite or resentment toward one another. There are many ways that sin gets in the way of true, perfect love. I'm sure you can share a few of your own...

However, there is a perfect, true love for us! That love is God! God is *love* (John 4:8)! He will never fail you nor forsake you (Hebrews 13:5). His love has no measure and can't even be fathomed with our little human brains! His love shows no bounds nor limits! He is waiting for you to accept His love—revel in it, lean on it, share it, overflow with it!

God's love is the greatest gift you could ever receive!

So when you are feeling let down by human love, or you feel depleted or lonely; when you've sinned or are ashamed...turn to your true love—God! Let His love fill you and comfort you!

# Lukewarm Coffee

I made coffee this morning. But then, I just left it sitting by my purse on the counter, and off I went to do my morning Bible study. Next, I woke my daughter up, made lunches, got us both ready for our day…and finally made it back for my coffee an hour later. It was cool, some of the coffee was settled at the bottom; it was even a bit bitter. It certainly did not serve its purpose for me this morning.

Just like this cup of coffee, sometimes, we set our faith aside. We go to church on Sundays. We are full of praise and God's love, motivated to go out into the world to tell others about Him and live out our purpose. But all too quickly, we walk away from our faith, our dedication to God's word, and our prayer life. We leave it countered just like a cup of coffee. And when we do that, we get cold, lukewarm in our walk with Christ. Even the truth we know (God's truth from His word) settles. We are easily swayed to believe society and follow the laws of man and not God.

When all of that happens, we can be confident that our purpose in Christ is not being fulfilled.

Is your faith like a strong hot cup of coffee? Or is it like a cup of coffee that's been pushed to the side and left to weaken and grow cold?

Do something about it! Get back into the word, be revived, pray, and seek Him in all you do. Just like how I'm going to revive my coffee in the microwave…

# Sit Still

I remember the summer after my daughter finished kindergarten. She was struggling quite a bit with her basic reading: phonics, sight words, letters, and sounds. So we put her in a tutoring center, where a couple times a week, they worked with her, but every night at home, we were supposed to work with her and complete certain pages of her workbooks. She would squirm, wiggle, bounce, sway...she simply could not sit still and focus. She was so easily distracted, and she struggled through every moment of these lessons. To be completely blunt and honest with you, it was pure torture for all of us!

This reminds me of one of my most favorite scriptures, Psalm 46:10, "Be still and know that I am God."

We are asked to be still and acknowledge our Lord as our Savior, our strength, our answer, our focus, our all in all. When we are still, we are submitting. And when we fully submit, when we are still and undistracted, only then can we realize the truth! We are able to soak in the fullness of God and who He is. We are focused on His power. We realize the battle has already been won. We see His presence in our life. We are able to let go so that He can be in control.

Those two little words—be still—carry such a deeper meaning. In the action (or lack thereof), we are able to be held and cared for by our Father in heaven.

Just like my little girl struggled to be still and to focus on her work, we have the same shortcomings in our lives. We struggle to be still and at peace and to open our eyes and our hearts to see God at work and allow Him to be in control. Take a moment right now and be still. Focus on our great God, who has all things in His capable hands, and revel in His love for you! Let go of your control, and let Him be God of your life.

# Imagine the Love
# of Christ...

His love for us is so strong, so unconditional, so deep, that we can't even comprehend it! The love that He offers us is accepting of us right now, this moment! No matter how messed up we feel, how lost, how useless, sin-filled...He loves you! His love doesn't grow stronger as you accomplish more. His love doesn't diminish when you make a bad choice.

Sit and think about that for a moment! What freedom does that bring? For someone like me who values people based on the accomplishments that can be made in a day, this is a *huge* breath of fresh air! I could go through this entire day and not accomplish one thing (the thought makes me sick to my stomach), but God would love me the same as He does right now! I don't have to earn His love. He doesn't value me based on what I do!

But...some might ask, "Then why do anything? Why even try to live a good life?" As Christ loves me, I love Him! Thinking about this love and the love (and gratitude) I have back for Him, makes me *want* to do good deeds in His name. We do what is right and try to share His love because of His love. I can glorify His name, praise, and serve Him by living a life *for* God!

Thank you, Lord, for such an amazing love!

# Stay in Your Lane

One of my husband's favorite (and most helpful) quotes is "stay in your lane." Wouldn't life be so much easier if we all would just stay in our lane? I was thinking about racing. Everyone starts out in their own little lane—a white line on both their left and right to keep them headed on the right path. But then, by the end of the race, everyone has moved, shifted, and shuffled until they all passed the finish line.

The truth of the quote "stay in your lane" is double-edged. Certainly, there are times when we do need to mind our own business. We need to stay out of the gossip! And we need to not compare our journey, our life, our bodies, our goals, and our successes to others. Comparison is the thief of joy. And "staying in your lane" can help you to avoid some unnecessary pain and frustration.

However, I can think of many times when Christians need to get out of their lane. In order to serve, to be hospitable, and to minister to others, sometimes, we must step into the path of another. Our lanes must overlap or intersect. What a sad life it would be if we could never cross paths with another person. Where would our worship and fellowship be? Where would our service and ministry be?

How do we know when to stay in our lane and when not to? That is called wisdom. It is listening to God's prompts and callings. Our decision to move outside of our lane happens when we hear and know the truth. God is our guide, our path. Pray and listen! Then trust God when you step across the white lines, into another lane.

# What's at the End of Your Finish Line?

> Let us throw off everything that hinders and the
> sin that so easily entangles. And let us run with
> perseverance the race marked out for us, fixing
> our eyes on Jesus, the pioneer and perfecter of
> faith. (Hebrews 12:1–2)

I've heard this verse or portions of this verse, and I've seen it on encouraging photos and on art, postcards, etc. I love it! Especially as a health and fitness coach, it connects even more with me. However, there is a portion of this verse that is often cut out or overlooked, and that is the portion I want to focus on.

When you are running a race (a real athletic race) you are usually keeping your eye on the finish line or looking toward that finish line. Your time is based on crossing that mark! Success comes when crossing the finish line.

In today's scripture, the focus of our eyes and our race should be on Jesus!

Fix your eyes upon Jesus! When you are living life, working hard, in the valley (meaning, a tough/challenging time), when you are living—fix your eyes upon Jesus!

Prior to saying this, it is written that we should throw off what hinders us and get out of the sin that pulls us back—that might get in the way of our race. But how do we do that? It comes when our eyes are on Jesus! So in this verse, we are learning that when our eyes are on Him, not only can we run a great race (meaning, work hard at whatever we are trying to accomplish for Christ or the challenges we must face in this life) but we can also avoid the hindrances and fight off sin.

It seems so simple, doesn't it? Keep your eyes on Jesus! But trust me, the devil loves to try to distract us. He is always trying to get us to take a moment away from Him. That is why prayer and reading your Bible are so important. When you pray and when you are in His word, those are the practices that help build your relationship with Christ and strengthen your focus on Him.

So as you run your race for today, keep your eyes on Him. Feeling distracted? Pray! Pull out your Bible (or one of the many Bible applications available now), and read! You can do this with God's help!

# Open My Eyes, Lord

God opened Hagar's eyes to see a well (of water), a well close by her home...

Hagar and her son were dying of thirst, yet there was a well—one that she had not known was there. She cried out to the Lord for help when she knew all hope was lost, and He opened her eyes.

Sometimes, we are blind to something in our life that is so clear, so obvious, right in front of us, but we cannot see it. When we look to God, focus on Him, and call to Him for our help and salvation, He reveals all. So often, our focus and our search are in the wrong place: inward.

We want to solve our own problems. We want to be the hero. We want to be self-reliant, important, independent, problem solver, in charge, leader, etc. We can do it on our own! And the amazing thing is, we start this fight for control and independence as little children at age 2-3! We've all seen toddlers struggling to do something by themselves! They crave independence as we do! It is part of our human nature.

But when our focus is on God, and He is in control (we give up our obsession with control and give it to God), we find peace. We find solutions, we find joy, we find humility, and we find a much better way to live. God reveals the well to us...we just have to trust in Him.

Ask God to open your eyes today and to help keep them trained on Him! That our struggles might end our peace, and joy may be filled!

# CONTINUALLY IS A
# TALL ORDER

Rejoice always, pray continually, give thanks in all circumstances; for this is God's will for you in Christ Jesus. (1 Thessalonians 5:16–18)

Rejoice *always!* Pray *continually!* Give thanks in *all* circumstances! Such short little phrases, but such a *huge* task. How do we rejoice when a loved one is sick, a child is lost, and our home is destroyed? How do we stay joyful when money is tight, our child is rebelling, and our marriage is struggling?

The third directive, give thanks, is the key to living a life of joy and prayer. When we give thanks for the little things in life (and the big things), it completely changes our perspective, our heart, and our ability to feel joy in spite of our external circumstances. No matter how bad life looks all around us, there are always things to be thankful for.

In the midst of the darkness, be still and thank God for the little things.

# Teach Your Children

After communion, I always pray. On Saturday, at an outdoor event at our church, we shared communion together as a fellowship. After drinking the juice and eating the bread, I prayed, as I always do. When I opened my eyes, this was the sight I saw: my daughter, head bowed, hands clenched together, eyes closed, praying hard! Tears welled up in my eyes at the beauty, peace, and prayer sitting before me.

Do you pray with your children? We need to teach our children to pray. Prayer is *so* important! Prayer is your direct line to God. It is the relationship builder and the way that we can communicate and be with God—in His presence. But it is learned.

Jesus even taught His disciples how to pray. Therefore, we need to be teaching and modeling prayer! When I was teaching in Lutheran schools, we talked about prayer a lot, and we prayed a lot! I always told my kiddos that praying is simply talking to our heavenly Father. There is no wrong way! We all have different prayer lives, and that is okay as long as we are praying.

There are so many amazing verses in the Bible that talk about prayer, and so many times when Jesus, himself, prayed! Share these verses with your children; read them yourself. Pray! Pray alone in quiet, but also pray with your children so that they might know and hear how important prayer really is.

Pray without ceasing. (1 Thessalonians 5:17)

Do not be anxious, but in everything by prayer and supplication with thanksgiving let your requests be made known to God. (Philippians 4:6)

Call to me and I will answer (Jeremiah 33:3)

# THIS TIME, THIS PLACE

I find myself wanting more, wanting new…what's next? What more can I be doing? What in my life needs to be changed or realigned? I just have that urge to do more, serve more, and live life better. And that isn't a bad thing, but sometimes, it can become a distraction from what God is trying to do in my life right now, in this moment. What if God is trying to use me today, but I'm so busy looking ahead to tomorrow that I miss His call, His nudge, or His whisper?

One of the most widely known, much loved scriptures about the life of Esther says it all, "Perhaps this is the moment for which you were created" (Esther 4:14).

God has me (and you) at the exact place we are meant to be. We need to be patient in His timing, His plan, and have complete faith in the fact that He is orchestrating our opportunities to serve Him and to fulfill our purpose in this life. Sometimes we are called to be still, enjoy the moment, or rest in the blessings of today.

> Be still before the Lord and wait patiently for him. (Psalm 37:7a)

It can be so easy to get rushed, to push forward, and to move on our own. But without the presence, the plan, and timing of God, it is for nothing. And we risk missing our true purpose. So today, listen for His prompting. Enjoy and be present in each moment. Don't go ahead of God.

> When the time is right, I, the Lord, will make it happen. Isaiah 60:22

# DISTRACTION!

I think the most effective tool the devil uses on me (and probably most of you too) is distraction! I start my morning in prayer, read devotions, and set my mind on God and the work He has for me each day. *But*...it doesn't take long for the devil to sneak some distractions into our lives, right?

Whether it's an iPad, Facebook, a person (yes, he even uses our family members to pull us away from our focus on God); the email saying your bank account is overdrawn; a meeting that doesn't go so well at work, or even something as simple as spilled milk. Anything to derail our thoughts and actions from the way we intend to live in Christ.

I often think about the fruits of the Spirit—these are virtues of a Christian walk with Christ. The Holy Spirit, within us, helps to supply them: kindness, goodness, self-control, patience, peace, love, joy, gentleness, and faithfulness. These are the things I aim for in my daily walk through life. And when I lose them and find bitterness, anger, frustration, depression, self-pity, etc. in their place, I know I've lost my focus. And I can just see the devil, on the sidelines, snickering, and gloating that he was able to pull me away.

The good news is that it only takes a prayer, a moment of thanksgiving or praise, and the invitation for the Holy Spirit to work inside me, that I gain my refocused walk with Christ. The devil never wins when you put your eyes back on Christ and His love, forgiveness, and mercy!

> I have given you authority to trample on snakes
> and scorpions and to overcome all the power of
> the enemy; nothing will harm you. (Luke 10:19)

# IDENTITY STARTS WITH THE CREATOR

In our culture, we often identify ourselves by our career. I know that "teacher" was always a definition I leaned on. Teacher defined me. I taught in the classroom for fourteen years and had dreamed of teaching from the age of nine. So teaching was fully ingrained in me. But when I left teaching (in the traditional sense) and took a year off to be a stay-at-home mom, I lost my identity. I felt so lost and unable to "find myself" or define myself. It was such a strange place to be, and I never realized how tied I was to the title "teacher."

So often, we rely on our jobs, our culture, our background, or even our family name to define who we are. But those things are just words, labels. They don't make us who we are. If your label is stripped away, what are you left with?

The first step in our journey of defining who we are or discovering our identity is to dig deep, to the core, to the beginning, to the Creator. I was created with purpose. I was created with love, in the image of my creator, God. I am His daughter (Jeremiah 1:5; Ephesians 2:10).

The foundation of our identity starts with knowing who the Creator is, that we are His masterpiece, and we are created with purpose.

Father God,

Thank you for creating me in a unique, purposeful way. You knew me and had a plan for me, even when you created the sea, the sky, the creatures, and the lands. You are the Creator, and you have a plan. Each day, Lord, I want to live for you—living out my purpose. Help me to rest in the comforting fact that I am a daughter of the King! Amen.

# THE WHOLE STORY

In the beginning, we were created in God's own image, carefully and wonderfully made.

But sin found its way into the world through the temptation in the garden; Eve ate the fruit forbidden by God.

The whole world is now overcome by sin, temptation is prevalent, and no one is above it but God.

The consequence for sin is death.

So God sent His son, Jesus, to earth.

Jesus lived a sinless life and took the punishment of death in our place.

He overcame death, the devil, and sin when He rose from the dead.

Our sin is now washed clean. It is erased.

We are not sentenced to death but promised eternal life.

There is a place set aside for us in heaven.

No pain, no tears, no sadness.

Only joy, worship, and peace in the presence of God.

What can you do to earn this eternity and relationship with the one true God?

Nothing! It is a gift.

Accept His forgiveness, His love, and Jesus as the Savior of the World.

Romans 6:23 reads, "For the wages of sin is death, but the gift of God is eternal life sin Jesus Christ our Lord."

# REFERENCES

2020. Dictionary.com. Accessed June 25, 2020. {https://www.dictionary.com/browse/home?s=t

# The Bible App.
# NIV Edition

www.biblegateway.com NIV Scripture used for searching scripture throughout my devotion writing journey.

# ABOUT THE AUTHOR

As a childhood leukemia survivor, Correne Constantino always knew God had a purpose for her life. Throughout her childhood, she felt called to be a teacher. After graduating from Concordia University in Portland, Oregon, she fulfilled her first calling: teaching at a Christian school in California. She spent the next fourteen years teaching in private and public schools in several states.

Correne is married to her best friend, Steve, and together they have a twelve-year-old daughter, Rylee. The little family relocated to Texas in 2016, and the calling to teach changed. Correne was called to a new mission within her community and a new job working at Zula B. Wylie Public Library in Cedar Hill, Texas. Over the past several years, she's been writing and sharing her devotions through social media as a way to inspire and share Christ day by day.

It has always been her dream to publish as a way to share Christ with others. This book is a work of praise to glorify the Lord and Savior, our Father in heaven!

CPSIA information can be obtained
at www.ICGtesting.com
Printed in the USA
BVHW071233190821
614776BV00007B/309